LEARNING ABOUT
Plants

Catherine Veitch

The author would like to dedicate this book to her mother,
Jacqueline Veitch, who inspired her with a love of nature.

Raintree is an imprint of Capstone Global Library
Limited, a company incorporated in England and
Wales having its registered office at 7 Pilgrim Street,
London, EC4V 6LB – Registered company number:
6695582

www.raintreepublishers.co.uk
myorders@raintreepublishers.co.uk

Text © Capstone Global Library Limited 2014
First published in hardback in 2014
First published in paperback in 2015
The moral rights of the proprietor have been
asserted.

Edited by Dan Nunn, Rebecca Rissman,
and Sian Smith
Designed by Joanna Hinton-Malivoire
Picture research by Mica Brancic
Production by Sophia Argyris
Originated by Capstone Global Library Ltd
Printed and bound in China by South China
Printing Company Ltd

ISBN 978 1 406 26608 5 (hardback)
17 16 15 14 13
10 9 8 7 6 5 4 3 2 1

ISBN 978 1 406 26613 9 (paperback)
18 17 16 15 14
10 9 8 7 6 5 4 3 2 1

British Library Cataloguing in Publication Data
A full catalogue record for this book is available
from the British Library.

Acknowledgements
We would like to thank Michael Bright for his
invaluable help in the preparation of this book.

We would also like to thank the following for
permission to reproduce photographs: Photoshot
pp.4 inset top, 24 thorn (© Imagebroker.net);
Science Photo Library p.4 inset bottom (Dr
Jeremy Burgess); Shutterstock pp.4 mian (©
Igor Normann), 5 (© Dave Head), 6 (© Galyna
Andrushko), 7 (© Panitchon), 8 (© Neirfy), 9 (©
szabozoltan), 10 inset (© de2marco), 10 main
(© Timolina), 11 (© Maxim Blinkov), 12 inset (©
Antonio Abrignani), 12 main (© Martin Fowler), 13
(© aodaodaodaod), 14 (© Serg64), 15 (© Sergey
Galushko), 16 inset (© Anest), 16 main (© ER_09),
17 (© saiva_l), 18 (© Gabriela Insuratelu), 19 (©
Katharina Wittfeld), 20 (© a9photo), 21 (© yuriy
kulik), 22 bud (© Serg64), 22 bulb (© de2marco),
22 flower (© Sergey Galushko), 23 fruit (© Igor
Normann), 23 leaf (© Sergey Galushko), 23 petal
(© Martin Fowler), 23 pollen (© Antonio Abrignani),
23 roots (© design56), 23 seeds (© Chepko Danil
Vitalevich), 24 seed pod (© szabozoltan), 24 stem
(© Dave Head), 24 vine (© Katharina Wittfeld).

Contents

Blackberry

thorn

fruit

roots

Bluebell

petal

stem

5

Bullrush

flower

stem

6

Cosmos

petal

stem

Freesia

bud

flower

8

Honesty

seed pod

seed

flower

bulb

10

Ivy

leaf

stem

Orchid

pollen

petal

Pitcher plant

leaf

Poppy

bud

stem

Rose

bud

leaf

thorn

15

Strawberry

seed

fruit

Sweet pea

petal

stem

stem

flower head

18

Tomato

fruit

vine

19

Venus flytrap

leaf

Water lily

flower

leaf

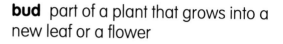

Picture glossary

bud part of a plant that grows into a new leaf or a flower

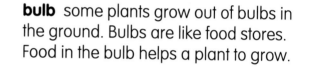

bulb some plants grow out of bulbs in the ground. Bulbs are like food stores. Food in the bulb helps a plant to grow.

flower part of a plant that makes seeds. The smells flowers make and their colours help to attract insects.

fruit fruits hold seeds. Plants make fruit so that animals will eat the fruit and carry the seeds to new places.

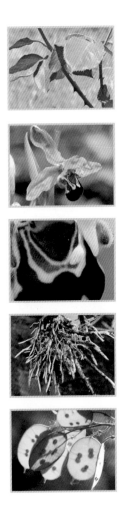

leaf part of a plant. Leaves use sunlight to make food for the plant.

petal one of the coloured parts of a flower

pollen powder inside a flower. Pollen has to move from flower to flower or plant to plant for plants to make seeds.

roots part of a plant that holds the plant in the ground. Roots bring water to the plant.

seed pod case that holds seeds and helps to keep them safe

seeds plants make seeds. Seeds grow into new plants.

stem part of a plant from which the leaves and flowers grow. Stems hold plants up and carry water to different parts of the plant.

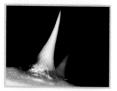

thorn hard, sharp point that sticks out from the stems of some plants. Thorns help to stop animals from eating the plant.

vine long, winding stem that creeps along the ground or climbs up things

Notes for parents and teachers

- Go on a nature walk with the children. Help them to identify different plants and their parts. Children can sketch or photograph what they see. Use the pictures to create a class book.
- Collect different flowers and leaves. Discuss the different shapes and colours of the flowers and leaves. Press the flowers and add these and the leaves to the class book. Remind children to always check with an adult that flowers and leaves are safe to collect, and to always wash their hands after handling flowers and leaves.